2012

PRAYING THROUGH A CHILD'S ILLNESS

28 Days of Prayer

Wessel Bentley

UPPER
ROOM BOOKS®
NASHVILLE

PRAYING THROUGH A CHILD'S ILLNESS: 28 Days of Prayer
Copyright © 2011 by Wessel Bentley
All rights reserved.

The Upper Room Web site: www.upperroom.org

UPPER ROOM®, UPPER ROOM BOOKS®, and design logos are trademarks owned by The Upper Room®, a ministry of GBOD®, Nashville, Tennessee. All rights reserved.

Scripture quotations are from New Revised Standard Version Bible, © copyright 1989 National Council of the Churches of Christ in the United States of America. Used by permission. All rights reserved.

Cover image: © Sean Justice / Corbis http://corbis.com
Cover design: Left Coast Design, Portland, OR / www.lcoast.com
First printing: 2011

LIBRARY OF CONGRESS CATALOGING-IN-PUBLICATION DATA
Bentley, Wessel.
    Praying through a child's illness : 28 days of prayer / Wessel Bentley.
        p. cm.
    ISBN 978-0-8358-1064-7
    1. Parents—Prayers and devotions. 2. Sick children.
    3. Intercessory prayer. 4. Prayer—Christianity. I. Title.
    BV4845.B46 2011
    242'.4—dc22   2011011195

Printed in the United States of America

ACKNOWLEDGMENTS

I would like to thank three groups of people who made this book possible. Needless to say, the first is my family: Natalie, Matthew, and Nathan. Your love, encouragement, and support through good times and bad bear testimony to God's work in our little "team." Second, thanks must go to Africa Upper Room Ministries and those who assist them. Specifically, thanks go to Roland Rink, Renny Stoltz, Thyrza Price, and Dion Forster for doing the first editing of the manuscript. Finally, thanks must go to the team at Upper Room Ministries, Nashville. Sarah Wilke, Robin Pippin, Joanna Bradley, Jeannie Crawford-Lee, and many others have done a wonderful job in putting together this edition of the book. God bless you all.

* * *

Dedicated to Matthew, our son.
Since birth
you reminded us of God's love.

CONTENTS

WEEK 3: WHAT CAN I DO?

WEEK 4: HOW DO WE LIVE?

INTRODUCTION

Events during the first year of our firstborn son's life inspired this book. What you are about to read is based on our experience and the experiences of others who have walked the road of caring for an ill child. You will see that there are no generic answers but simply thoughts and prayers that helped us through difficult times. Allow me to briefly share our story with you.

For two years Natalie and I had been trying to conceive without success. You can imagine our joy when the doctor phoned, saying, "You are going to have a baby!" We were ecstatic. Just when we thought that all hope was lost, it happened. We were going to have a baby! Not only would this child be our first, but he or she would be the first grandchild on both sides of the family. Grannies started knitting, grandpas talked about taking this child on fishing trips. This child was not only going to be our child but also would belong to the whole family.

Weeks and months passed and, with the doctor, we agreed that this little boy, who would be called Matthew, would be delivered via caesarean section on September 11, 2003. We chose to give Matthew an unofficial second name, Nkosinathi. "Matthew" means "gift from God," and "Nkosinathi" means "God is with us." We couldn't have imagined how much these names would mean in the months and years that followed.

Matthew Nkosinathi Bentley was delivered on the morning of September 11, a Thursday morning. Everything appeared to go well with the procedure. Matthew emerged, a seemingly healthy little boy, screaming at the top of his lungs. I will never forget his face, all wrinkly, with his eyes barely open. The doctors and nursing staff quickly took him away to be weighed and to do the necessary checks. Then, without any comment, they charged with him to the neonatal intensive care unit. He was turning blue, a sign of lack of oxygen. Natalie was heavily sedated and did not know quite what was going on. I stood feeling helpless and all alone. What were minutes felt like hours.

The medical team first thought something was wrong with Matthew's lungs; they inserted drainage pipes, but this did not help. A cardiologist arrived; after a prolonged ultrasound, she called me aside. Matthew had severe heart defects, she told me. His aorta and pulmonary arteries were switched around, a condition called Transposition of the Great Arteries (TGA). There were big holes in the septum, which separates the atria and the ventricles. The heart was twisted and was positioned on the opposite side of his chest. The chances for Matthew's survival were slim.

That evening I went home, expecting a telephone call telling me that Matthew had passed away. When Natalie woke, she was wheeled to the ICU to see our little child, covered with pipes, drips, and probes. She had a chance to hold him, but not for very long because his body was frail.

The next morning came, but no telephone call. Matthew was still frail but seemed to be stabilizing. Days passed and he seemed to be getting slightly stronger. We started a conversation with the cardiologist, who indicated that it was possible for Matthew to undergo surgery. It would be risky because several interventions would be necessary. Matthew would in all likelihood not live a normal life, but we were informed that these interventions might offer him a fair quality of life, if he survived. Matthew was first discharged from hospital three weeks after his birth, but he had to return to hospital several times after that. At four months old, Matthew was admitted to the Sunninghill Hospital as a patient in the Walter Sisulu Paediatric Cardiac Centre. Given his frailty, the doctors had decided to try to fix everything in one go. Our baby underwent an eight-hour operation on January 22, 2004.

Matthew was discharged a week later and has since been extremely healthy. Thus far he has not needed further surgery and is as active as all his peers, a gift we thank God for every day. Every time we remember the journey we have been on, we know God has been with us. There were times of great uncertainty, not only regarding Matthew's health but also concerning finances, fear of the unknown, and anxiety about what the future might hold.

In the years since, we have traveled a similar road alongside several families. Being a minister, I see these situations arise frequently, and every time I glimpse back into our own history. I write this book still with raw wounds but with hope that these reflections and prayers will be a source of encouragement to you and your family. Every child's story is different, every family's journey unique. I do not offer concrete answers or pretend that I can fully understand your history. These meditations and prayers are for parents and families who seek encouragement. I simply pray that you experience God's peace and comfort during this difficult time.

HOW TO USE THIS BOOK

The twenty-eight days of prayer are divided into four weeks, each week centered around a theme. Each seven-day cycle ends with a sabbath, so start your weeks on a Monday. Sabbath offers a time for rest and reflection. On that one day set all things aside to focus on your place with God and to give thanks.

Begin each day's reading by taking a minute to reflect on the topic of the day. What does this mean to you? What goes through your mind when you are faced with the thought the topic suggests? Next, read the Bible text for the day. Read the passage slowly. Take note of words or phrases that stand out for you. Ask yourself what the scripture has to say about the topic. Then read the meditation.

These meditations represent reflections on the Bible passage and on the topic that helped Natalie and me as we grappled with our own questions. Each meditation leads to a prayer that starts with the words "Almighty God." I have used this form of addressing God intentionally. In times when we feel weak, it is important to acknowledge that there is One on whose name we can call; this God is more in control than we are. Feel free to make the prayer your own. Fill in the blank lines with your own words.

Finally, consider the Suggestion that accompanies each meditation. Each Suggestion presents a practical way you might bring the topic, scripture, meditation, and prayer into your own situation.

I pray that these meditations, prayers, and suggestions will bring you strength, comfort, and the assurance of God's presence with you.

WEEK 1

How Can This Be?

MONDAY
The shock of knowing

Read Psalm 121:1-2.

There is no more numbing experience than finding out something is wrong with your child and you can do little about it. It feels like a bad dream, and you wish that you could suddenly wake up with the great relief that it was not real. But you don't. Reeling from the enormity of the situation, you ask one question: *What now?* The small trickle of this question grows into a torrent of *Why? How? Who?* and *When?* It is easy to get lost in these questions, like a person who suddenly, without explanation, finds himself or herself in the middle of the wilderness, trying to make sense of what is and what should be. Join the psalmist in this barren place: "I lift up my eyes to the hills—from where will my help come?"

Don't rush to answer this question. A Christ-follower might be tempted to respond with the following verse (verse 2) in the form of a cliché. Don't jump to this concluding answer. Instead, allow God to minister to you in the midst of your confusion. Let God's voice permeate through the darkness of this cloud; wait for God's presence to reach you through the fog that prevents you from seeing beyond this point.

What is God saying to you? Take some time with this meditation. Read verse 1 over and over again, until such time that verse 2 reflects what God wants you to hear.

Prayer

Almighty God, my child is ill. I stand stunned by what I've heard. We were told that . . .

....

....

....

....

This is beyond my control. It is more than I can handle. Lord, please answer me! Where will my help come from? Amen.

Suggestion

Allow yourself to feel whatever emotions rise to the surface. If you want to cry, then do. If you feel angry, then be angry. If you feel at a loss, then simply hold this feeling in your heart. Try to surround yourself with people whom you love and trust, people who will allow you the space to express your feelings.

TUESDAY
Feeling exhausted

Read Psalm 121:4.

How do you feel today? Take a moment to reflect on this question. Be honest with yourself and perhaps voice your feelings aloud. "Exhausted" may be one feeling you name.

Emotional stress is extremely tiring. It is hard to rest, even to allow yourself to sleep or to take a short nap. Perhaps you believe that you need to stay awake, aware of everything that happens. Being alert gives us a sense of control; we may even believe nothing will happen as long as we stay awake.

Today's reading served as a source of strength to us in the midst of Matthew's struggle. It reminded us that God never sleeps. We are human, our bodies are frail, and we tire; but this passage assures us that we have a God in whom we can trust. When we fall asleep, God stays awake.

It may be difficult at first, but surrender your resting time to God. You may want to return to this meditation from time to time. Allow God to take some control, even if it is just during the time when you need to rest. As you do, you may find it easier to trust God with more and more. God never sleeps. God is awake when you are not. God is holding your hand and your child's hand while you take time to recuperate.

Prayer

Almighty God, when I need to take a rest, I feel . . .

....

....

....

Please give me the assurance that you are indeed the God who never sleeps. Help me to come to that place where I can trust you with my child's well-being while I am restored through rest. In Jesus' name I pray. Amen.

Suggestion

Plan some time to rest today. You can do this by asking a friend or family member to stand in for you while you retreat. You may even want to speak to your physician about getting assistance to help you sleep.

WEDNESDAY
Does God care?

Read Matthew 19:13-15.

One of the most difficult questions to answer for yourself is *Does God care?* Does God really care about our child, and if so, how can God allow our child to be this ill?

Friend, I do not have the answer to this latter question, and anyone who offers a simple solution to this complex problem might not comprehend that he or she is speaking on God's behalf—something we as human beings simply cannot do.

There is encouragement in this passage from Matthew, and I believe it answers the first question. Jesus said, "Let the little children come to me." Pause here for a moment. Reflect on these words. Repeat this phrase today as a point of meditation. In my mind's eye I imagine Jesus surrounded by children. He bends down to meet them where they are, to look them in their eyes, and to have his ears close to their mouths. He embraces them, loves them; they feel secure and at ease.

How would you react today as Christ seeks to be with your child? Perhaps you think you need to protect your child from God, but look at this passage again. Jesus' love for the children speaks for itself. I hope that you will sense his presence with you and with your child today. As you sit next to your child, Jesus is there, crying with you while saying to your little one, "Don't worry, I am here."

Prayer

Almighty God, it is so hard to understand how you care about our child when our little one is so ill. It doesn't make sense. When I read this passage, I would like to believe . . .

....

....

....

Help us all to find your peace and hear your inviting voice so that we, as your children, can come to you unhindered. Amen.

Suggestion

Spend time with your child, praying for him or her. Be open in your conversation with God. See Jesus standing beside you. Talk to him about how you love this child and hear the Spirit's affirmation that God loves you and your child too.

THURSDAY
Why?

Read 1 Corinthians 13:12.

"Just wait, you'll see," my grandfather told me. I was about five years old and had dropped a flashlight. The top came off, the bulb shattered, and the batteries spilled all over the floor. I thought that the flashlight was broken. No matter how much I tried to put all the pieces together, it simply wouldn't work. My grandfather walked into the room and picked up all the pieces. On the way to the garage, where he kept all kinds of spare parts, I kept apologizing but also tried to convince him that he was wasting his time. The flashlight was, in my opinion, beyond repair. "Just wait, you'll see." I probably don't need to tell you how the story ended.

This passage from Corinthians reminds me of that day. There are three parts to this verse. First, we are reminded that we cannot always see how things are going to work out. Second, it tells us that the Christian journey is one where God, who knows how all things will unfold, accompanies us on our journey. And last, we can conclude that because this God knows us intimately well, God will minister to us in ways that we understand.

You and I may not be able to answer the question *Why?* but take heart today knowing that God sees further than we are able to see. The Christian faith assures us that God breaks through our situations of pain and is able to transform our places of despair into spaces of hope. Can you trust God with your child today? God loves you and your child. When things do not make sense to you, draw strength from the promise that the God who sees all things is the One holding your hand.

Prayer

Almighty God, I don't know why things happen. I haven't been able to find anyone who does. So I turn to you, for you are able to see things I cannot. Lord, I want to ask *why*. Why . . .

....

....

....

Help me to be patient and to be here for my child. And help me to understand how you are walking beside us on this difficult road. Lord, can you give us assurance that this situation is in your hands? In Jesus' name I pray. Amen.

Suggestion

Ask your medical caregiver about a support group for parents who have or who are experiencing a situation similar to yours. In such groups you are able to speak to people who understand your situation but see it from a different perspective. Listening to others also enables you to understand you are not alone.

FRIDAY
Gaining clarity

Read Philippians 2:1-2.

During our son's illness, Natalie and I received wonderful gifts of love, support, and compassion from the doctors and nurses. Along with these gifts, the medical staff offered time—time to talk and to ask questions. They were able to answer some questions, but at times the best response they could give was "We do not know." They enabled us to gain a degree of clarity about the journey we were on. While we wanted to be able to see around that elusive corner, we came to understand that we can project into the future only so far, often not far enough to predict an outcome.

The medical staff displayed God's gift of love in action by being there to respond to what at times may have seemed demands for healing. This was something they could not promise, but their openness and honesty facilitated the healing process in our hearts and minds. Their responses prepared us emotionally and mentally for the journey ahead. And so, part of our Christian walk during this time was spent praying for the doctors and other caregivers. We thanked God for their knowledge. We thanked God for their abilities. Prayers were offered that they would not only do the best they were able to offer but also that, as they listened to us, God would speak through them the words we needed to hear. Certainly these were not always words we *wanted* to hear, but in retrospect, God used their honesty to allow us to embrace the reality of what we were dealing with.

Prayer

Almighty God, today we give thanks for the doctors and caregivers who are helping our child. We thank you for . . .

....

....

....

Lord, today we want to ask them about . . .

....

....

May they speak with honesty and clarity, which will help us gain a picture of the road ahead. Amen.

Suggestion

Ask your doctor or caregiver if you can spend some time in an open conversation about what is taking place. Prepare yourself for this conversation by drawing up a list of areas in which you would like to gain clarity.

SATURDAY
The gift of listening

Read Genesis 2:1-3.

A lot has been said during this past week. And you have listened. People have spoken words of support. Medical staff have conveyed their thoughts and understanding. Your family may have had conversations on simply how to cope. Undoubtedly many voices have competed for a place of prominence in your mind. Among these a sentence or a word may have stood out: something you want to hold on to as a source of strength. Friend, let me ask: have you had some time to listen to the stillness of God's voice?

Perhaps draw aside tonight and look up to the heavens. You don't have to say anything. You don't have to pray. Think about the vastness of the universe, the way in which God set each star and planet in its place. Listen. Look. Marvel. Make time for silence and solitude. As you behold the glory of creation, be reminded that it is this Creator God who is journeying with you and your child. What is God saying in your spirit?

Tomorrow will be the seventh day of this prayer journey. As you will see, there is no meditation but a few suggestions for reflecting on the past week. Take this time to rest in God. Find time to breathe deeply, to gather strength, but most of all to hear God's voice. Remember that even when you try to find time to gather yourself, God does not sleep or slumber. God, Creator of the universe, is there for you and is the source of your strength.

Prayer

Almighty God, when I look to the heavens, I know that you are much bigger than I can ever imagine. At times our troubles seem so big. It often leaves me feeling . . .

....

....

....

Holy Spirit, remind me of your awesome power. Allow me to hear the gentle voice of God speaking to me in moments of quiet. Amen.

Suggestion

Take some time to be alone, where you can be quiet and are able to focus on God. You may want to try the idea mentioned in the meditation: take a walk outside tonight and gaze at the sky's expanse. Bring your worries to God who created all of this and who remains in control of it all.

SUNDAY
Celebrate God's Faithfulness

As you journey through today, focus on how God has been faithful to you, your child, and your family during the course of this week.

Give thanks for the following:

- Your family
- Your friends
- The doctors and medical caregivers who share their gifts with you
- The way the community has shown support
- Your place in nature
- Your place with God

Write down some thoughts concerning your journey this week.

WEEK 2

Whom Can I Blame?

MONDAY
Is it God's fault?

Read Psalm 22.

Lord, couldn't you have prevented all this? This prayer, I'm sure, is prayed several times a day. If God is God, then surely God must be in control of all things, especially the health of a child.

In Archibald MacLeish's play *J.B.*, based on the book of Job, the character Nickles expresses doubt about a God who allows suffering:

> If God is God He is not good,
> If God is good He is not God . . .[1]

Is God to blame for your child's ill health? Like the psalmist, we sometimes come to the point of asking whether God has forsaken God's people. Sometimes it certainly feels like it. Jesus quoted this psalm while on the cross. The pain we feel and the questions we ask are real. They are not meant out of spite or expressed with malicious motives. Where is God in all of this?

As you read through Psalm 22, take note of how the psalmist discovers the presence of God. The psalm ends almost opposite to its beginning, but we sense that the psalmist would not have come to this point if he had not been completely honest about his emotions and dared to ask the questions that were haunting him. God is big enough to hear our tough questions. God is also big enough to help us understand God's presence by using language and images familiar to us. Why not take time to ask God those tough questions? Let God know exactly how you feel. My prayer is that as you give these words and questions to God, you will experience God ministering to you in the midst of your pain.

Prayer

Almighty God, there are times when I feel very angry with you. There are questions in my mind that are unanswered and that I cannot understand. Let me ask you . . .

....

....

....

Help me to come to the same conclusion as the psalmist, that you do "not despise or abhor the affliction of the afflicted," that you do not hide your face but hear when I cry to you (Ps. 22:24). Amen.

Suggestion

As you journey through this day, keep Psalm 22:24 close to your heart. Dare to ask God your questions. Let this verse remind you that God has not turned away from you but is present and truly hears your prayer.

TUESDAY
Was it me?

Read John 9:1-12.

You can't help but ask whether you could have prevented the suffering of your child. When I shared the news of Matthew's condition with my family, some thought that they were to blame. They quoted texts like Exodus 20:5: "I the LORD your God am a jealous God, punishing children for the iniquity of parents, to the third and the fourth generation of those who reject me."

In the scripture passage today, the disciples must have the same verses in mind when they ask about the source of this man's condition. But Jesus sets the record straight: "Neither this man nor his parents sinned" (John 9:3). Jesus presents the people with a picture of God who is neither vindictive nor malicious; God shows compassion and is filled with love.

It would seem impossible to worship a God who takes out frustrations on innocent children. God is not fighting against you. Even if you have issues to rectify with God or with others, God's presence will not focus on what you have done wrong. The divine focus is on God's ability to journey alongside you, ministering to you in times of need. May this day be filled with a sense of release—release from guilt, shame, anger, and resentment. Remember, God is with you. If you need to reconcile with God or with others, seek to do so today. God is not the threat but the one who offers shelter, a place of respite when life is at its most difficult.

Prayer

Almighty God, at times I feel to blame for my child's illness. There is something that wants to make me believe I have acted wrongly and you are punishing my child. These places of brokenness come to mind . . .

....

....

....

Lord, heal me today from these perceptions. May I know you as the God of love and not a god of malice. In Jesus' name. Amen.

Suggestion

As you journey with this text today, remind yourself and those around you that God is a God of compassion and love. Rather than enforcing retribution, God always seeks the path of grace. Can you remind yourself of other places in the Bible where God showered people with compassion and grace? Reflect on your own life and remember when God showed love when you might have expected otherwise.

WEDNESDAY
Is it the devil?

Read Romans 8:37-39.

Here is a thorny question: is it the devil? On the one hand, it would be easy to attribute the suffering of the innocent to a force or spirit that stands in opposition to God. On the other hand, we live in a world where more and more is explained through our knowledge of the universe.

While we do not want to give the devil too much credit for things gone wrong, we would be foolish to deny the existence of evil. In C. S. Lewis's *The Screwtape Letters*, Screwtape (a senior devil) writes to his young nephew: "If once we can produce our perfect work . . . the man, not using, but veritably worshipping, what he vaguely calls 'Forces' while denying the existence of 'spirits'—then the end of the war will be in sight." [2]

We may not be certain of the answer to this question about the devil, but we can be sure that Christ's love can overcome anything that challenges our lives. Even if fear, uncertainty, and anxiety fill your day, know that these experiences cannot barricade God's love from reaching you and lifting you above your distress. The devil simply is not that powerful. Our God is God, and nothing in this universe can change that. So place your life in the hands of the Almighty. Rest in the embrace of God, for no evil—however big—will be able to breach the security of God's affection.

Prayer

Almighty God, thank you for scripture that reminds us that evil is neither big enough nor strong enough to surmount the vastness of your love. Lord, I sometimes doubt your greatness when I feel . . .

....

....

....

I pray with all the Christ-followers through time: "Deliver us from evil." Amen.

Suggestion

Write the words "Nothing can separate me from God's love" on a piece of paper. Carry this with you during the day and remind yourself of this fact whenever you feel insecure. You might also make a card with these words for your child. As you pray for your little one, remind her or him too that God's love cannot be broken or overshadowed.

THURSDAY
What about the doctors?

Read Mark 9:17-18.

"Can't they do more?" The father's frustration in this Bible passage is familiar. He probably had heard about Jesus and hoped that he would heal his son. At first he couldn't meet Jesus personally, so the next best thing was to seek help from Jesus' followers. To the father's dismay, they weren't able to heal the boy.

Why do we often feel frustrated with doctors, thinking that they aren't doing enough? Perhaps it is because the world has come to see doctors as "miracle workers," and so we expect them to have all the answers. Certainly medicine has improved and continues to do so on a daily basis, and some medical interventions border on the miraculous. But at the end of the day we need to acknowledge that doctors and caregivers can know and do only so much. They are people who have answered God's call upon their lives to care for others to the best of their ability. When they don't have the answers we expect, we may feel they have failed, just as people thought the disciples did not do enough that day.

Instead of being frustrated with what may seem to be medicine's limitations, I encourage you today to pray again for the medical caregivers who are looking after your child and your family. Pray that they may grow in knowledge. Also pray and trust that the Great Physician, the One in whom you can place your hope, is the One who inspires them to minister to you and your little one.

Prayer

Almighty God, when I consider what the doctors are doing, I am sometimes plagued by the thought that they are not doing enough. In my mind, I think they should be trying . . .

....

....

....

I pray for them today that they may be inspired and so fulfill the gift of healing that you have given to them. Amen.

Suggestion

Have you had time this week to speak with your child's medical caregivers? Last week you were encouraged to be in conversation with them. When you create time for questions, you may discover that everything you thought they should be doing is being addressed already.

FRIDAY
Where is the church?

Read Acts 2:43-47.

There is no substitute for knowing that you belong among people who truly care about your well-being. You can have all the riches of the world or even all knowledge, but knowing you belong is priceless. Today's scripture pictures the early church as a community in which people worshiped God by caring for one another.

Have you let your faith community know about your difficult journey? Perhaps you could share your concerns about your child with one or two people who worship with you. Sharing heartaches with others is a risk, and understandably it may not be your first course of action, but you never know who God may send to draw alongside you. Someone sharing as little as a prayer could make a difference. There may be individuals who have experienced something like what you face right now; they will understand what is in your heart and on your mind.

We are approaching the end of the second week of this journey, and the sabbath is coming. Have you thought of spending time in worship with others? You will know if you are ready for this, but I encourage you to share with God's people and to allow the body of Christ to minister to you and your family. After all, if one suffers, the entire body suffers. If one finds shelter, the entire body experiences peace.

Prayer

Almighty God, you have called your church to serve and love those who are in need. Lord, my needs are . . .

....

....

....

Inspire your church, your people, to be facilitators of wholeness and peace in our lives. May we hear your voice of comfort speak through your people and so come to know that we belong. Amen.

Suggestion

Have you spoken to your minister or church community about your needs? Make a point today to be in conversation with someone who can accompany you and your family in prayer. It is reassuring to know others can pray for you when you do not have the strength to pray.

SATURDAY
Elusive peace

Read John 14:23-27.

In today's Bible reading Jesus comforts his disciples and reminds them that the Spirit's presence will always accompany them. Verse 27 stands out. Peace in the midst of trouble is something we all hope for, but that can seem impossible when your mind is occupied with something else, especially the ill health of your child.

Reading this passage, you may think Jesus is being unreasonable in saying, "Do not let your hearts be troubled, and do not let them be afraid" (John 14:27). *Lord, how can I not be troubled or afraid?* It is a natural response. Friend, I don't think Jesus asks you to deny feelings or emotions. Jesus certainly does not want you to respond stoically to what affects your loved ones or deal with people in distress in a matter-of-fact kind of way.

Listen to what Jesus says. God offers peace in the midst of the storm. Sometimes this peace is tangible. At other times, you may feel far removed from this place of comfort. God can offer peace because the situation is in God's hands.

In that moment when you feel you have reached the end of your tether and cannot be in control anymore, this verse speaks to you: "Peace I leave with you; my peace I give to you" (John 14:27). Pray with your family and with your child, and may the peace of the Lord be with you.

Prayer

Almighty God, I wake up thinking I have lost control of this situation. I feel tossed around by life itself. In this place where I have no control, I fear for myself, my family, and my child. I am worried about . . .

....

....

....

Let me hear your voice, Lord Jesus, speaking to me and my family, reminding us that God is here. Speak to us in ways we understand so that we will come to know the peace of God, which is greater than any other. In Jesus' name. Amen.

Suggestion

What reminds you of God's perfect peace? Do you find God's peace in nature? Perhaps you find God's peace through a hobby or interest. Spend some time in these places or in these activities and allow God to remind you of God's peace.

SUNDAY
Celebrate God's Presence

Matthew 28:20 reminds us that we will never be far from God's presence. Reflect on this past week.

Give thanks for the following:

- God's presence with your family
- God's presence with your little one
- God's presence through friends
- God's presence through the medical caregivers
- God's presence through the church
- God's peace that comes with God's presence

Write down some thoughts concerning your journey this week.

....

....

....

....

....

....

WEEK 3

What Can I Do?

MONDAY
Can I do anything?

Read Jeremiah 1:4-8.

How can I be there for my child? What can I do to make things easier? You want to do something, anything, everything, but feel so powerless. This text from Jeremiah shows how God can reach into the places of uncertainty and powerlessness and can awaken the ability to be a gift to others.

When God came to Jeremiah that day with this calling, Jeremiah became acutely aware of his own inability. As a response, Jeremiah gave the reasons why he could not serve. Then God reminded him of who he was. Jeremiah was known to God before he was born. God knew his strengths and his weaknesses, and God would become his source of strength in order to minister to the community.

Do you feel out of your depth as you wonder how God could use you to be there for your child? Read this portion of scripture again. Put yourself in Jeremiah's place. God has known you since before you were born. God knows your strengths. God knows your frailty. God can speak to you, touch your lips, and enable you to be an instrument of love and security to your child. Perhaps you are not convinced. Jeremiah wasn't either, but as he gave himself to God, God was able to use him, and Jeremiah became a source of God's voice to many.

Prayer

Almighty God, when I look at my child I feel so helpless. There should be something I can do to help [*Name*] know that your love is here. I feel unable to do this because . . .

....

....

....

Speak to me, Lord. Touch my lips, my hands, and my heart. Amen.

Suggestion

Today, don't put too much pressure on yourself to provide solutions, to have answers, or to be other people's source of strength. Spend time with God, and ask what you can do to be a gift to your child. God may ask you simply to be present and to listen. God knows how to use you best during this time.

TUESDAY
When I feel weak

Read 2 Corinthians 12:7-10.

Paul shares with the church in Corinth that something in his life kept him from feeling completely at peace. We do not know for sure what this problem was, but we sense that it caused him significant discomfort and led him to wrestle with God on numerous occasions, asking God that it be removed. Paul felt weak because of this disturbance. Furthermore, he believed his ability to serve God was being hampered by his weakness. Then he expresses a surprising thought: God's strength comes through particularly when we are weak and vulnerable.

Carrying on from yesterday's meditation, it is important to know when and where we feel weak and not to think that God can use us only when we are confident and strong. Draw hope from Paul's comments. When we feel disempowered, God is open to conversation, even when we ask challenging questions. At the same time, God shows compassion and grace and allows us to catch a glimpse of God's hand at work through our weakness.

We are now journeying through the third week. During this time, have you been able to perceive God speaking to you through your child, even in the midst of his or her illness? I pray that today you will find at least one moment when you will know the sufficient grace of God. Hold on to this moment and remember it when you find yourself in times of struggle and doubt. It is in the remembrance of God's faithfulness, even when we are weak, that we find hope and the ability to put one foot in front of the other. Divine strength be with you today in the moments when you feel weak.

Prayer

Almighty God, am I strong enough to cope with all that is happening? Do you think that I have the capacity to go through . . .

....

....

....

I am reminded through Paul's testimony that you do not require me to be strong at all times. In fact, it is in my moments of weakness that I can be certain of feeling your strong but gentle arms carrying me. In Jesus' name. Amen.

Suggestion

When you feel weak, take time to focus on your breathing. Force yourself to breathe slowly. Relax and repeat this phrase to yourself: "God is strong in this moment." This statement does not mean that God is forceful or demanding but that God can steer this ship when you feel you can't.

WEDNESDAY
Allowing others

Read Psalm 40.

You cannot do everything by yourself. Have you recently felt that you need to be in charge, make all the decisions, take the lead, and have the final say in almost everything? It is natural to try to take control when you feel absolutely out of control. There is no greater sense of powerlessness than when you have to face the reality of your child's struggles.

In today's reading, the psalmist invites us to explore the place where we can trust in God. We are not to surrender responsibility to make decisions or to care. Instead, the psalm leads us to understand that we are not alone in our responsibilities and duties.

How does God care for us? In short, divine love seems to reach us primarily through others. God empowers the caregivers, and so we can learn to trust their guidance. God cares through the church, and so we can trust that the prayers of those around us are heard. God inspires family and friends to help us make decisions and to work through our questions, and so we can trust that God's love speaks through them too.

It may seem like taking a risk, but what about praying today that you will know God's love and support through people around you? When people bless you with their gifts, you can trust that it is God at work. If you try to carry everything alone, you will soon become weary and unable to be the gift to others. Trust God and discern

God's will as you make yourself available to be blessed by others. We carry one another's burdens and bring strength to those who are in need.

Prayer

Almighty God, when I feel out of control, I have this desire to take charge without trusting anybody but myself. Lord, this especially happens when . . .

....

....

....

I trust in you today and believe that you send people into my life who are willing and able to be your signs of love and comfort in time of need. In your name I pray. Amen.

Suggestion

Take a moment today to place all the planned events and decision-making moments into God's care. Pray that God will send the right people to care for you and to assist you as you journey through this day. At the end of the day, read Psalm 40 again and give thanks for the ways in which God has shown faithfulness.

THURSDAY
When all I can do is pray

Read Matthew 6:5-8.

Thomas à Kempis wrote, "The devout man has Jesus with him everywhere to be his comforter, and to him he says: 'Be near me, Lord Jesus, always and everywhere.'"[1] These are moving words and indeed a prayer we can carry with us wherever we go. Although we have the assurance of Christ's presence with us at all times and in all places, there are moments when we know we cannot engage the world without withdrawing from it. Journeying with a child who is ill is not easy. It demands our attention, love, and self-giving. A person cannot give continuously without running dry. This is the place where all we can do is pray.

Prayer does not refer to a monologue with God but to a time when we not only speak but, most of all, have the opportunity to listen to God. Jesus describes this kind of prayer and offers insights into how we can find renewal through prayer.

First of all, draw aside: find a time and place where you can be by yourself without interruptions. Second, don't feel pressured to say anything to God, for God already knows what is in your heart. Third, dare to be honest when you speak with God: allow your feelings and emotions to find expression. You do not have to be politically or theologically correct; God is big enough to understand where you come from and why you say certain things. Finally, be quiet and listen, trusting that your prayer is heard. Being in the presence of God in open conversation is God's gift to you.

Prayer

Almighty God, you know that at times during these past weeks I prayed without ceasing and at other times I have had nothing to say to you. Lord, I commit myself to draw aside today to be in prayer. I plan to do this . . . (*include place and time*)

....

....

....

Today belongs to you, and I pray that you will protect this time for me, so that nothing will hinder me from finding renewal in your presence. Amen.

Suggestion

Write down the prayer from Thomas à Kempis or try to memorize it: *Be near me, Lord Jesus, always and everywhere.* As you journey through today, pray this prayer in preparation for your time away with God.

FRIDAY
When I cannot pray anymore

Read 1 Kings 19:9-13.

Elijah could not pray anymore. In the passage preceding the one for today, we find Elijah in the desert, hoping that all, including his life, would come to an end. Some would say that Elijah was trying to escape his reality, attempting to find a way out of dealing with the stresses and anxieties that his future held. Elijah did not have the strength to go to God anymore. The sad reality is that when we find ourselves in Elijah's position, we believe the only way to be in fellowship with God is for us to take initiative: we must pray, read our Bibles, and be strong in our faith.

God surprised Elijah, and I hope God will surprise you today. When Elijah could not go to God, God came to him. God met Elijah in the desert, not in the Temple. Elijah found a place of shelter, a cave, and here Elijah did the human thing: he attempted to find God in everything. Then God surprised him again by speaking through an unexpected source.

My prayer for you is that God will surprise you by appearing in the places where you try to hide from your fears. I pray too that you will find God leading you to a place of shelter where God can care for you. And I pray that you will hear God speaking through the unexpected. After Elijah was met by God and spoken to, he found renewed strength to continue with his life and calling. As you minister to your child and to your family, may you know God's strength and intervention.

Prayer

Almighty God, I get overwhelmed, and I wish that everything were just a bad dream that would come to an end. I hide to try to cope. I hide from . . .

....

....

....

Lord, meet me in the desert, lead me to a place of shelter, and speak to me. Surprise me by how you do that. In Jesus' name. Amen.

Suggestion

Allow yourself to hide today. When you hide, do not seek God but wait for God to find you. As you experience God's hand at work, record this moment by writing it down. Recalling this time may very well become a source of strength when you find yourself in the desert again.

SATURDAY
Equipping myself

Read 1 Samuel 17:40.

You know the story of David and Goliath. This verse has special significance for me, especially when faced with a difficult situation. A few years ago, Natalie and I, along with a group from church, had the privilege of going on a pilgrimage to Israel. We stopped at the Valley of Elah, where this historic confrontation took place. The stream mentioned in the text was no longer there. Instead, a dry riverbed with thousands of water-washed pebbles lined the ground. I imagined for a moment Goliath standing in the valley, and I pretended to be David, bending down to collect some stones. The stones certainly didn't seem to be a sufficient solution to the threat, but the story tells us otherwise. Today, one of those stones sits on my desk as a constant reminder of how God can use simple things to achieve great success.

With what will you equip yourself as you face the daunting task of dealing with your child's illness? Perhaps read up on the condition and possible treatments, speak to the doctors and caregivers, or simply sit with your child for some quality time.

In the bigger picture, the skills, knowledge, or tools with which you equip yourself may seem insignificant, perhaps insufficient, but allow God to use what you have as instruments of encouragement and strength. Remember that, at the end of the day, it was not the stone that overcame Goliath but David's willingness and obedience. God moved David to act with courage and self-preparation. God be with you as you face Goliath today.

Prayer

Almighty God, there stands Goliath. For me, Goliath is . . .

....

....

....

Lord, when I try too hard to be in control, it is like putting on armor that I cannot carry. Guide me in discovering the small and simple things that will prepare me for this journey. May these become the instruments through which my family and I cope and find wholeness again. Amen.

Suggestion

Take some time to walk around outside. Look at the ground, imagining yourself in David's place. Pick up a little stone, and let it symbolize God's ability to use seemingly small tokens of preparation. Let this stone remind you of God's faithfulness and presence.

SUNDAY
Celebrate God's Ability

At the end of the third week, take time to look back and see how God has interacted with you, spoken to you, and acted in love and faithfulness.

Give thanks for the following:

- God's ability to use you
- God's ability to provide strength in moments of weakness
- God's ability to use other people
- God's ability to hear your prayers
- God's ability to meet you and equip you when all seems lost
- How has God journeyed with you during the course of this week?

....

....

....

....

What are some of the life lessons you would like to carry with you into this coming week?

....

....

....

....

....

WEEK 4

How Do We Live?

MONDAY
One day at a time

Read Matthew 6:25-34.

Living one day at a time is easier said than done. You may have received the news that your child's condition will affect the lives of your family indefinitely. This reality is frightening, because you do not know how you will be able to put one foot in front of the other. The saying "take one day at a time" seems like a meaningless cliché, but draw strength from what Jesus teaches in today's passage.

By worrying about tomorrow or the future that lies ahead, you will not be able to change anything. This doesn't mean you should not prepare for what is to come. Today's scripture suggests that while you may have all the fears of the future at the back of your mind, the moment that needs your attention and commitment is *now*. Your child needs you today. Your family needs you today.

Jesus promises his followers that God knows our every need, even the needs that we worry about. God's strength will come to you today in just the right measure so that you can focus on the concerns of the present. Look at your child. For him or her there is only the present, and that is where you are needed.

So, yes, take each day as it comes. Each day may have new challenges, but through the power of God, there also will be new victories. Strength to you as you face today, knowing that the Lord is holding your hand.

Prayer

Almighty God, when I think of the future, I get anxious. I am scared of . . .

....

....

....

Lord, you are the One who is in our past, our present, and our future. You know what tomorrow holds. Help me to focus on today and to gain strength from the knowledge of your eternal presence so that the difficulties our family faces may be transformed into victories. Amen.

Suggestion

Don't try to suppress your worries. Attempt to face them head-on. Write these down and sit with your spouse, family members, or friends and pray through this list of worries, surrendering them into the hands of almighty God.

TUESDAY
Our daily bread

Read Psalm 91.

One sentence in the Lord's Prayer reads: "Give us today our daily bread." Continuing on from yesterday's thoughts, we learn from this line that God will give us enough grace and strength for our immediate needs. Psalm 91 is another source of strength and encouragement. We may ask how God knows our needs, and this is a very real question. By reading the psalm we become aware that God is able to know our needs because God is in this situation with us. Surrendering each day into God's hands gives us the same level of conviction as that of the psalmist: we can pronounce to the world that we are wrapped in God's wings (verse 4) and that nothing can penetrate the shielding love of God.

Have you observed how a bird protects its young? A bird shields its offspring from the cold, drives away immediate dangers, and provides sustenance. When reading Psalm 91, I can almost imagine God in this picture—God being the bird and we being the chicks. Our wings may be frail and our knowledge of the world and all it holds may be very limited, but there is One who looks out for us.

Why not pray Psalm 91 at the start of each day? Seek to live each day as its own unique moment, trusting that God's wings enfold you, your little one, and your family. God can bring comfort to your family and bring your daily bread in order that you may find enough strength to face each day.

Prayer

Almighty God, nature reminds me how you take care of every living being, giving to each according to its need. Lord, today my needs are . . .

....

....

....

I trust in your enfolding love and know that I am in your embrace, not because of anything that I may have done but because I am your child. I pray today again for my family and especially my child, that we may gain our daily bread and so testify of your providence. Amen.

Suggestion

Psalm 91 is a beautiful celebration. Why not take your Bible and read this psalm to your child? Read it to your family and remind one another that God's loving embrace is even in this moment. Hold on to God, for God will never let go of you.

WEDNESDAY
Entrusting God with the future

Read 1 Thessalonians 5:16-18.

You may have found, looking back over the past weeks, that you have, in fact, been praying without ceasing. C. S. Lewis asks a question we all wonder about: "What sort of evidence would prove the efficacy of prayer?"[1] He suggests that many people answer this question by counting the times they have received exactly what they have asked for. These moments, in all honesty, are not as frequent as we would hope for. God has a way of answering our prayers in different ways. God may even surprise us with an answer to a prayer that we did not pray aloud or consider to be significant.

We can be certain that God hears our prayers. We hold on to this belief, trusting that God is able to provide an answer, based on God's knowing our paths ahead. We may speculate about the future, but God is already in every possibility of every moment that we move toward. The struggle with prayer is caught up in the question *What must I pray for?* When we don't find an answer, it is easier not to pray at all.

Have you ever asked God what you need to pray for? Consider whether there is a place in your prayer life for the Spirit's guidance. Part of entrusting your future to God would be to simply ask where God wants you to focus, not only in your preparation but also in your prayers. God knows your journey, your child's journey, and all the possibilities that lie ahead. By praying and conversing with God, you are not shooting up aimless prayers, hoping that something may come of them. When you pray, you are in communion with the God who holds all eternity. Therefore, seek God's Spirit, converse honestly and openly, knowing that your prayers are heard.

Prayer

Almighty God, why does it seem at times that you are as uncertain about the future as I am? I may tend to treat you that way in the manner in which I pray, listen, and engage with you. It is hard to know that you hear my prayers, because . . .

....

....

....

Lord, remind me of your eternal nature. Grant me faith to know that even when I do not receive exactly what I ask for, you answer with the knowledge of my path ahead. Amen.

Suggestion

Have you ever kept a prayer journal? It might be good to write down some of the matters you pray about. In time, you can review the journal and see how God has responded.

THURSDAY
Faith

Read 1 Corinthians 13:13.

Paul names three pillars—faith, hope, and love—that support people's lives from day to day. Over the next three days we will explore how faith, hope, and love provide a framework for living.

What is faith? Society and even some churches promote the idea that faith is the belief in something that we wish for. We often hear the admonition to visualize a certain outcome and then hope for it without entertaining any doubt. This kind of blind faith leads to disillusionment when expectations do not come to fruition.

Perhaps faith is not as future-centered as we may think but depends more on our past. Why do I say this? Well, we have faith in people with whom we have journeyed; we have faith in processes from which we carry experiences and memories. Faith is not staring blindly into the future; instead, it is our knowledge from the past informing our belief for the future. Someone can easily tell you to have faith, meaning "hope for the best." That is not what scripture teaches. Time and again, the people of Israel were instructed to remember their history, to tell the stories to their children and their children's children. This remembrance cultivated faith; when the Israelites found themselves in a situation of uncertainty, their reflection on the past gave them courage to face their future.

Yesterday's Suggestion proposed starting a prayer journal. Try journaling again today. Remember your life story up to this point and the ways God has walked with you. Allow this recollection to become your source of faith for the future.

Prayer

Almighty God, when I remember my family's story up to this point, these events of your presence stand out . . .

....

....

....

Help me remember these stories and share them with others so that we may all grow in faith and in the knowledge of your Being. Amen.

Suggestion

Talk with your spouse or a friend about memories of God's actions during the past four weeks. How did God prepare you for what you have gone through? How has God spoken to you through your child, and what message of faith can you share? Tell your child the story of how God has been present.

FRIDAY
Hope

Read 1 Corinthians 13:13.

Where faith looks at our stories and builds the gift of courage for the present, hope is that which we dream about, based on these reflections. Just as faith is not aimless wishing, so hope is not aimless dreaming. We can never be certain about the future, but God does not stop us from trying to form a picture or an ideal of what we long for, both for ourselves and for others. If we only reflect on the past without projecting ourselves into the future, we may get tied up in the past, unable to move ahead.

It may seem like a daunting task, but have you and your family shared where you hope to be in a week's time? What about in a month or even in a year? Be careful not to make these hopes a perceived reality, using the kind of blind faith we spoke of yesterday. Dare to dream, hoping in faith and knowing that God (who is in our past as well as in our present and future) will guide your thinking and your actions. If God could share hopes for your future, what would God say? Are your hopes in line with what you think God is hoping?

Hope gives you something to move toward; it provides purpose and aim. You may even ask your child what he or she is hoping for. Include these hopes in your conversation with God and allow God to speak to you about decisions you need to make and responsibilities you need to fulfill as you make your way through this challenging time.

Prayer

Almighty God, there are certain things we hope for as we move from today. In faith and in the knowledge that you hear our prayers, we offer to you . . .

....

....

....

Lord, these are not aimless dreams. Enlighten our hearts and minds that we may discern your will for us and align our hopes with the future toward which you are calling us. Amen.

Suggestion

Talk to your family members about their hopes. Talk to your child about his or her hopes. Write these down in your prayer journal. These stories of hope, offered to God in prayer, may very well become the source of faith that you may require in the future. Dream big, hope with humble extravagance, and offer these dreams and hopes to God.

SATURDAY
Love

Read 1 Corinthians 13:1-13.

Faith reminds us of our past. Hope speaks to our future. It seems like Paul anchors the present to the gift of love. We cannot live exclusively either in the past or in the future. The present does not vacillate between the past and the future, between faith and hope. I hear Paul saying through this text that the best we can do in the present is to love. Friend, I am certain that love is the best gift you can give to your child. It is the best gift you can give to your spouse and your family. What is this love?

This passage describes love with characteristic attitudes and actions. Try replacing the word *love* in this passage with your name. Does the passage describe you in any way? I am sure many of these phrases do, but we all have room for growth. If you are in doubt about how to deal with arising situations, put on the spectacles of love and allow love to become the instrument through which your faith and hope find expression in the present.

From the beginning of these meditations, I've said there are no blanket answers to cover every situation—life does not allow for such generalizations—but love certainly levels the playing field. My prayer is that you will know the presence of God through remembering your encounters, hoping for the future, and acting in love as you cope from day to day. This is how we celebrate life.

Prayer

Almighty God, I am yours. We are yours. Help us to remember. Help us to hope. Help us to love. Help us to pray. I offer this prayer again for my family and for our child . . .

....

....

....

We know you hear our prayers. Amen.

Suggestion

May today be a day of thanksgiving. Give thanks for love that has been shown to you, your family, and your child. Give thanks for all God's people who make love a priority in their lives.

SUNDAY
Celebrate the Gift of Life

God has given the gift of life so that it may be lived in the full knowledge of God's commitment, love, and compassion.

Give thanks for the following:

- The ability to live one day at a time
- God providing what you need at the right times
- God being in your past as well as in your future
- The stories of God's faithfulness
- The gift of looking forward
- God's gift for the present, the gift of love

Write down some thoughts concerning your journey this week.

....

....

....

....

....

....

CONCLUSION

Friend, I know that this road is not easy. It is a path we do not choose for ourselves. My prayer for you is that you will find comfort and strength, living each day and finding courage to move forward. My further prayer is that the great cloud of uncertainty you faced at first when having to deal with your child's condition has dissipated and that you are more certain about the road ahead.

I invite you to go through these meditations again. More importantly, go through your memories and notes as you journeyed through each meditation. What were your thoughts at the time? What were you experiencing?

Reflecting on your journey will build memories and shape a story that you can tell to others concerning God's love, compassion, and faithfulness.

With much love and prayer,
Wessel Bentley

REFLECTION QUESTIONS

The questions provided here are designed to facilitate conversation. These are based on the content of each week's meditations. You are invited to journey through the entire week before working through these questions. The questions provide an avenue for sharing, discussion, and healing.

Week 1: How Can This Be?

1. Share your feelings with others as you remember the moment when you found out that all was not well.

2. Resting is not easy during times of stress. What advice has helped you find moments of recuperation?

3. Look again at the passage for Wednesday. Does this picture of Jesus resonate with you? Be honest in your reflection. Allow space for those who simply cannot see Jesus being open to embracing small children.

4. The question *Why?* is not new. As you prayed the prayer, asking God this difficult question, what response from the Spirit did you sense?

5. Knowledge empowers. What information has assisted you in gaining clarity about your child's condition and the road ahead?

6. God does not always tell us what we want to hear. Share with others what you desperately wanted to

hear. Also share what was said. Is there something from your conversation that you needed to hear?

7. How has God been faithful to you and your family during these past seven days?

Week 2: Whom Can I Blame?

1. Do you feel God is responsible, even partially, for your child's ill health? Have you been able to speak honestly to God about this? How has that helped?

2. What makes you think that you are to blame for this situation? Minister to one another as you search for peace.

3. Sometimes we have the perception that the devil is just as powerful as God. What do you learn from the passage on Wednesday this week about the extent of God's ability to love you and your family?

4. Doing your own research may lead you to believe the doctors have not thought of something critical. Share with one another how you will make time to discuss options with the medical caregivers.

5. To belong gives us a sense of being connected and cared for. Discuss ways the presence of the family of God may have supported you.

6. In what ways have you found peace, especially when feeling overwhelmed?

7. Knowing God cares for you can be a source of peace. How have you sensed God's presence?

Week 3: What Can I Do?

1. When and where did you feel powerless during this past week? To what small temptations in your life are you unable to say no?

2. How have you witnessed God's strength during the moments when you couldn't do anything?

3. People are God's instruments of love. Spend some time in prayerful conversation giving thanks for the gifts people have shared with you this week.

4. You may have experienced hours and days when you did not stop praying and also times when you could not pray. Describe times when you could not pray.

5. The story of Elijah in the desert is a reminder of hope. God pursues us even in our moments of distress. Where has God found you in distress?

6. Has God revealed to you how to equip yourself for the road ahead?

7. God is able to do all things. We can only do so much. How do you hold these two faith truths in balance?

Week 4: How Do We Live?

1. Name what makes it hard for you to focus on the present. How can you make sure you are in your child's present—where he or she needs you most?

2. God gives us just enough to see us through every situation of need. What stories can you tell of God's providence? Share with one another.

3. Can you trust God with your future? What makes it difficult to let go?

4. Tell the story of your journey so far to others. Listen to them as they share their stories or the same story from a different perspective. What faith lessons emerge from these stories?

5. Share your dreams and hopes with those around you. How can they support you as you work toward these hopes?

6. To love one another is the perfect gift in the present. Read 1 Corinthians 13:1-13 aloud, replacing the word *love* with your name. Affirm one another through these words.

7. Remember *faith*, *hope*, and *love*. How can reflecting on these pillars of Christian life described by Paul shape your journey ahead?

NOTES

1. Archibald MacLeish, *J.B.: A Play in Verse* (Boston: Houghton Mifflin, 1958), 11.
2. C. S. Lewis, *The Screwtape Letters: With Screwtape Proposes a Toast* (London: HarperCollins, 2002), 31–32.

WEEK 3

1. Thomas à Kempis, *The Imitation of Christ*, trans. Betty I. Knott (London: Fount, 1996), 118.

WEEK 4

1. C. S. Lewis, *C. S. Lewis on Faith*, comp. Lesley Walmsley (London: HarperCollins, 1998), 56.

ABOUT THE AUTHOR

WESSEL BENTLEY, an ordained minister in the Methodist Church of Southern Africa, is a part-time lecturer in the Department of Philosophy and Systematic Theology at the University of South Africa. He holds a Bachelor of Theology degree from the University of South Africa and three degrees (B.A. [Honors], M.A., Ph.D.) from the University of Pretoria. He is working toward an honors degree in psychology at the University of South Africa.

Wessel and his wife, Natalie, have two sons and reside in Pretoria, South Africa. Follow Wessel on Twitter and at his blog:

on Twitter @wesselbentley
http://www.wesselsplace.blogspot.com

ALSO BY WESSEL BENTLEY

- *Facing Financial Struggle: 28 Days of Prayer*

- *The Notion of Mission in Karl Barth's Ecclesiology*

- *What Is a Good Life? An Introduction to Christian Ethics in 21st Century Africa,* ed. by Louise Kretzschmar, Wessel Bentley, and Andre van Niekerk

- *What Are We Thinking? Reflections on Church and Society from Southern African Methodists,* ed. by Dion Forster and Wessel Bentley

- *Methodism in Southern Africa: A Celebration of Wesleyan Mission,* ed. by Wessel Bentley and Dion Forster